Practical LENORMAND

Meanings & Combinations of the 36 Cards

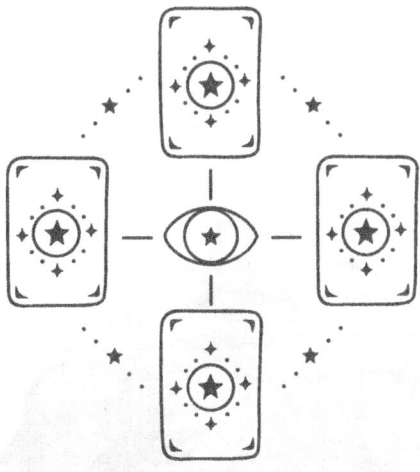

LAURA BAUMANS

Copyright © 2024 LAURA BAUMANS
All rights reserved. Any reproduction, even partial, of this work is prohibited. Any copy or reproduction by any means whatsoever constitutes an infringement punishable by the penalties provided for by the law of March 11, 1957 and the law of July 3, 1985 on the protection of copyright.
ISBN : 9798340339997

SUMMARY

INTRODUCTION

PART ONE:
Meanings and Combinations of the 36 Cards

1- Rider....................................8
2- Clover..................................10
3- Ship....................................12
4- House..................................14
5- Tree....................................16
6- Cloud..................................18
7- Snake..................................20
8- Coffin..................................22
9- Bouquet...............................24
10- Scythe...............................26
11- Whip.................................28
12- Birds.................................30
13- Child.................................32
14- Fox...................................34
15- Bear.................................36
16- Star..................................38
17- Stork.................................40
18- Dog..................................42
19- High Tower.........................44
20- Garden..............................46
21- Mountain...........................48

22- Path 50
23- Mouse 52
24- Heart..54
25- Ring...... 56
26- Book 58
27- Letter 60
28- Mister...62
29- Lady...6
30- Lily..66
31- Sun 68
32- Moon 70
33- Key 72
34- Fish 74
35- Anchor 76
36- Cross 78

PART TWO:
Reading Models

Line Reading 82
Cross Reading 84
Column Reading 85
Triangle Reading.............................86
Global Reading 87
Intuitive Reading 88
Large Reading Board 89

Introduction

This practical manual of the **Petit LENORMAND oracle** is suitable for **beginners as well as the more experienced**. **Easy to use**, it contains the **essentials to help you get started in the divinatory** arts and also allows you to deepen your knowledge.

The Meanings and Combinations of the 36 cards, in the first part, reveal the symbolism of each card and the associations with two cards. So during your draws, you can refer to them and they enlighten your interpretations.

In the second part, you will find several **Complete Reading Models**. Simple and accessible, they guide you in a predictive approach and develop your intuition through practice. They are adapted **to all areas of your life: love, professional or material**.

After you have familiarized yourself with the deck and the meanings of the cards, the last part is devoted to **creating your own Large Reading Board Lenormand**.

Doing readings is about taking time for oneself, reflecting on our desires and emotions. Alone or with others, it gives you the opportunity to express yourself about personal situations. It is important to consider **the readings as entertaining and to maintain your free will**.

PART ONE

MEANINGS AND COMBINATIONS OF THE 36 CARDS

1- RIDER
NINE OF HEART

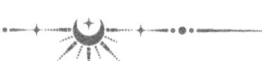

MEANING OF THE CARD

The Rider is the bearer of news. It can be someone coming to us, a messenger. It symbolizes the joints, the knees and the feet. The event happens quickly.

The Rider and other cards

Rider – Clover 2: luck arrives.
Rider – Ship 3: person moving away.
Rider – House 4: visit to the home.
Rider – Tree 5: energetic visitor.
Rider – Cloud 6: visitor creates discord.
Rider – Snake 7: visitor causes tensions and jealousy.
Rider – Coffin 8: visitor in mourning; with House, it means a family death.
Rider – Bouquet 9: happy visitor.
Rider – Scythe 10: unwanted visitor.
Rider – Whip 11: quarrelsome visitor.
Rider – Birds 12: talkative visitor.
Rider – Child 13: visit of a child, pregnancy.

Rider – Fox 14: job change.
Rider – Bear 15: financial windfall.
Rider – Star 16: calm, serene visitor.
Rider – Stork 17: visit from a woman who is a mother; with Moon, it's your mother.
Rider – Dog 18: a friend visits.
Rider – High Tower 19: administrative visit.
Rider – Garden 20: visit from a group.
Rider – Mountain 21: distant visitor.
Rider – Path 22: visitor arrives.
Rider – Mouse 23: visitor doesn't arrive.
Rider – Heart 24: visit from a lover.
Rider – Ring 25: marriage announcement or family visit.
Rider – Book 26: secret visitor.
Rider – Letter 27: news arrives.
Rider – Mister 28: a man brings news or receives news.
Rider – Lady 29: a woman brings news or receives news.
Rider – Lily 30: proper and distinguished visitor.
Rider – Sun 31: pleasant visitor.
Rider – Moon 32: troubled visitor.
Rider – Key 33: a solution is found.
Rider – Fish 34: professional change for independent work.
Rider – Anchor 35: assurance that the visitor arrives.
Rider – Cross 36: unhappy visitor.

2- CLOVER
SIX OF DIAMOND

MEANING OF THE CARD

The Clover announces luck, happiness and success. It represents the general state of the person. The event takes place between one and six weeks.

The Clover and other cards

Clover – Rider 1: lucky visitor.
Clover – Ship 3: positive trip.
Clover – House 4: lucky home.
Clover – Tree 5: serenity, happiness.
Clover – Cloud 6: passing worry.
Clover – Snake 7: jealous and lucky.
Clover – Coffin 8: end of a lucky period.
Clover – Bouquet 9: luck and well-being.
Clover – Scythe 10: abrupt end to serenity.
Clover – Whip 11: luck that brings misfortune.
Clover – Birds 12: luck that brings gossip.
Clover – Child 13: lucky child.
Clover – Fox 14: a job that brings a lot of money.

Clover – Bear 15: luck due to chance.
Clover – Star 16: luck and tranquility.
Clover – Stork 17: luck creates change.
Clover – Dog 18: lucky friend arrives.
Clover – High Tower 19: administration gives a chance.
Clover – Garden 20: luck with friends, socially.
Clover – Mountain 21: obstacle to luck.
Clover – Path 22: choice of the lucky path.
Clover – Mouse 23: wasting luck.
Clover – Heart 24: lucky love.
Clover – Ring 25: lucky union.
Clover – Book 26: secret luck.
Clover – Letter 27: announced luck.
Clover – Mister 28: lucky man.
Clover – Lady 29: lucky woman.
Clover – Lily 30: luck and distinction.
Clover – Sun 31: luck and well-being.
Clover – Moon 32: illusory luck.
Clover – Key 33: problem solved.
Clover – Fish 34: luck in work.
Clover – Anchor 35: preserved luck.
Clover – Cross 36: end of a lucky period due to misfortune.

3- SHIP
TEN OF SPADE

MEANING OF THE CARD

The Ship represents a foreign or free person. It announces a journey or a small trip. The Ship speaks of the liver, the spleen or the beer gallbladder. The period is very close, speed.

The Ship and other cards

Ship – Rider 1: arrival of a foreign person.
Ship – Clover 2: lucky move.
Vessel – House 4: family travel and with the stork it means a move abroad.
Ship – Tree 5: journey of comfort, relaxation.
Ship – Cloud 6: unsettling, disturbing journey.
Vessel – Snake 7: distrust of a foreign person.
Ship – Coffin 8: end of a journey.
Ship – Bouquet 9: pleasant journey.
Ship – scythe 10: travel, movement cancelled.
Ship – Vhip 11: journey that creates conflict.
Ship – Birds 12: discussions regarding a move.

Ship – Child 13: a child's journey.
Ship – Fox 14: working abroad or remotely.
Ship – Bear 15: money coming in from abroad.
Ship – Star 16: mystical Journey.
Ship – Stork 17: journey Abroad.
Ship – Dog 18: foreign friend.
Ship – High Tower 19: consulate or Embassy.
Ship – Garden 20: friend Abroad.
Ship – Mount 21: journey blocked or delayed by obstacles.
Ship – Path 22: travel by car.
Ship – Mouse 23: impossible journey because too expensive.
Vessel – Heart 24: distance from spouse.
Ship – Ring 25: honeymoon or union abroad.
Ship – Book 26: secret voyage.
Ship – Letter 27: news from abroad.
Ship – Mister 28: a foreign or independent man.
Ship – Lady 29: a foreign or independent woman.
Ship – Lys 30: serene journey.
Ship – Sun 31: journey to the Sun.
Ship – Moon 32: travel causes fear, nervousness; imaginary travel.
Ship – Key 33: solution found abroad.
Ship– Fish 34: travel for independent work.
Ship – Anchor 35: big opportunity.
Ship – Cross 36: unfortunate move.

4- HOUSE
KING OF HEART

MEANING OF THE CARD

The House represents a good, warm, helpful man; the home or family. Something that lasts over time. Signifies prosperity and stability.

The House and other cards

Home – Rider 1: a visit home.
House – Clover 2: luck in the home.
Home – Ship 3: home Abroad.
House – Tree 5: serenity in the home.
House – Cloud 6: conflicts in or about the home.
House – Snake 7: family members are jealous of our home.
House – Coffin 8: illness or death in the house.
Home – Bouquet 9: joy in the home.
House – Scythe 10: break with family ties.
House – Whip 11: family quarrel.
Home – Birds 12: discussions in the home.
Home – Child 13: family home; renewal in

the hearth; project for a house.
Home – Fox 14: work from home.
House – Bear 15: home with abundant finances.
House – Star 16: serene home.
House – Stork 17: moving.
House – Dog 18: loyalty and friendship in the home.
House – High Tower 19: retirement home, institutions; with the moon psychiatric hospital.
House – Garden 20: social and friendly prosperity.
House – Mount 21: obstacle in the home.
House – Path 22: choice to be decided as a family or regarding a property.
House – Mouse 23: theft or worries in the home.
House – Heart 24: house filled with love.
House – Ring 25: happy and united home.
House – Book 26: secret House.
House – Letter 27: news about a house.
House – Mister 28: warm and understanding man; brings security into the home.
House – Lady 29: warm and understanding woman; brings security into the home.
House – Lys 30: house where righteousness and goodness reign.
House – Sun 31: happiness, success in the home.
House – Moon 32: psychological problem and depression in the home.
Home – Key 33: solutions to family problems.
House – Fish 34: owner, real estate agent or builder.
House – Anchor 35: deep family attachment.
House – Cross 36: unhappy at home.

5- TREE
SEVEN OF HEART

MEANING OF THE CARD

The Tree is a sign of physical and mental strength, vitality and health. It also represents a healthy young girl; patience and longevity. The time corresponds to one year.

The Tree and other cards

Tree – **Rider 1:** healthy visitor.
Tree – **Clover 2:** luck and vitality.
Tree – **Ship 3:** healthy movement.
Tree – **House 4:** serene and healthy home.
Tree – **Cloud 6:** temporary lung problems.
Tree – **Snake 7:** intestinal problems.
Tree – **Coffin 8:** healing.
Tree – **Bouquet 9:** health and joy.
Tree – **Scythe 10:** dental problems.
Tree – **whip 11:** joint problems.
Tree – **Birds 12:** healthy conversations.
Tree – **Child 13:** healthy child.
Tree – **Fox 14:** medical work.

Tree – Bear 15: healthy finances.
Tree – Star 16: serene climate.
Tree – Stork 17: healthy change.
Tree – Dog 18: childhood friend.
Tree – High Tower 19: good health; healthy institution.
Tree – Garden 20: healthy social circle.
Tree – Mount 21: severe health problems.
Tree – Path 22: healthy choice.
Tree – Mouse 23: drug taking, addiction.
Tree – Heart 24: healthy feelings.
Tree – Ring 25: healthy union.
Tree – Book 26: healthy situation.
Tree – Letter 27: news about your health.
Tree – Mister 28: stable, serious and healthy man.
Tree – Lady 29: stable, serious and healthy woman.
Tree – Lily 30: righteousness and serenity.
Tree – Sun 31: perfect health.
Tree – Moon 32: depression, psychological problems.
Tree – Key 33: finding the right treatment.
Tree – Fish 34: healthy self-employment.
Tree – Anchor 35: excellent health.
Tree – Cross 36: poor health.

6- CLOUD
KING OF CLOVER

MEANING OF THE CARD

Symbol of imbalance, instability and confusion. The Cloud also represents a wise and old man; as well as the eyes. The period is in autumn or on a passing time.

The Cloud and other cards

Cloud – Rider 1: worried visitor.
Cloud – Clover 2: temporary luck.
Cloud – Ship 3: distancing following a conflict situation, passing event.
Cloud – House 4: temporary family inconvenience.
Cloud – Tree 5: allergy, asthma.
Cloud – Snake 7: defamation, gossip.
Cloud – Coffin 8: respiratory problem.
Cloud – Bouquet 9: short-term worries.
Cloud – Scythe 10: immediate decision.
Cloud – Whip 11: temporary problems.
Cloud – Birds 12: stormy discussion.
Cloud – Child 13: dissipated child.

Cloud – Fox 14: temporary work; trouble.
Cloud – Bear 15: financial worries.
Cloud – Star 16: unusual fact.
Cloud – Stork 17: brief complication.
Cloud – Dog 18: trouble with a friend.
Cloud – High Tower 19: complication with the momentary administration.
Cloud – Garden 20: concern with a social circle.
Cloud – Mount 21: prolonged worry.
Cloud – Path 22: choice to make following a temporary concern.
Cloud – Mouse 23: financial worries.
Cloud – Heart 24: emotional worries.
Cloud – Ring 25: temporary quarrel in the couple.
Cloud – Book 26: secret concern.
Cloud – Letter 27: bad news.
Cloud – Mister 28: a worried man.
Cloud – Lady 29: a worried woman.
Cloud – Lily 30: hypocrisy, falsehood.
Cloud – Sun 31: temporary anxiety.
Cloud – Moon 32: psychological instability; depression.
Cloud – Key 33: solving a problem.
Cloud – Fish 34: worry at work.
Cloud – Anchor 35: long-lasting worry.
Cloud – Cross 36: sadness, misfortune, mourning.

7- SNAKE
QUEEN OF CLOVER

MEANING OF THE CARD

The Snake is an interested, hypocritical person; a slanderous, frivolous woman; of good advice who brings help. It symbolizes jealousy, lies, betrayal; the intestines. It is a period of waiting, of transformation.

The Serpent and other cards

Snake – Rider 1: visit from a worried person; insincere.
Snake – Clover 2: luck makes people envious.
Serpent – Ship 3: abnormal distance.
Snake – House 4: jealousy, hypocrisy in the home.
Snake – Tree 5: intestinal problems.
Snake – Cloud 6: gossip.
Serpent – Coffin 8: sexual disease; end of a betrayal, of a transformation.
Snake – Bouquet 9: happiness makes people envious.
Snake – Scythe 10: breakup, end of ambiguous relationships.
Serpent – Whip 11: violence, aggression.
Snake – Birds 12: slander.

Snake – Child 13: mean, jealous, envious child.
Snake – Fox 14: hypocrisy at work.
Snake – Bear 15: financial lie.
Snake – Star 16: woman disturbs serenity.
Snake – Stork 17: accused by a mother.
Snake – Dog 18: hypocritical friend.
Serpent – High Tower 19: brothel; adult site.
Serpent – Garden 20: social hypocrisy.
Serpent – Mount 21: big worry, danger.
Serpent – Path 22: making the right choice in his relationships.
Snake – Mouse 23: dispute and quarrel following a lie.
Snake – Heart 24: emotional betrayal.
Serpent – Ring 25: infidelity.
Serpent – Book 26: secret vice.
Serpent – Letter 27: false news.
Serpent – Mister 28: fickle, hypocritical man and liar.
Snake – Lady 29: fickle, hypocritical woman and a liar.
Snake – Lily 30: distrust, deception.
Snake – Sun 31: favorable sexual opportunity.
Snake – Moon 32: anxiety, uncertainty and fear.
Serpent – Key 33: a lady brings the solution.
Snake – Fish 34: bad partner at work.
Snake – Anchor 35: jealousy, infidelity that lasts.
Snake – Cross 36: misfortune due to bad relationships.

8- COFFIN
NINE OF DIAMOND

MEANING OF THE CARD

The Coffin ends a difficult situation and speaks of transformation. Symbolizes a sorrowful spirit, mourning; infinity.

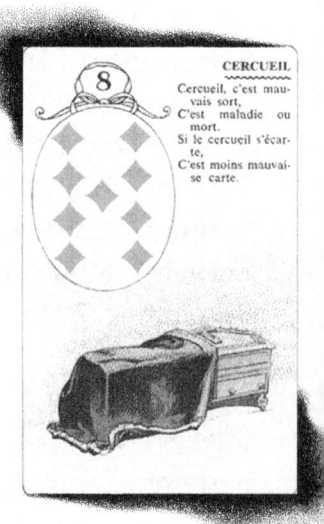

The Coffin and other cards

Coffin – Rider 1: sick visitor or announcement of a death.
Coffin – Clover 2: end of a bad streak.
Coffin – Ship 3: death of a person abroad, far away.
Coffin – House 4: illness or death in the family.
Coffin – Tree 5: healing.
Coffin – Cloud 6: lung disease.
Coffin – Snake 7: painful disease that destroys.
Coffin – Bouquet 9: return to happiness.
Coffin – Scythe 10: accident or surgery.
Coffin – Whip 11: painful illness, feet, knees.

Coffin – **Birds 12:** nervous, psychiatric illness.
Coffin – **Child 13:** sick child.
Coffin – **Fox 14:** end of a job.
Coffin – **Bear 15:** inheritance or donation.
Coffin – **Star 16:** skin problem.
Coffin – **Stork 17:** gynecological problem.
Coffin – **Dog 18:** sick friend, deceased.
Coffin – **High Tower 19:** hospitalization; isolation.
Coffin – **Garden 20:** need for solitude.
Coffin – **Mount 21:** serious illness.
Coffin – **Path 22:** leg pain, blood circulation.
Coffin – **Mouse 23:** osteoarthritis.
Coffin – **Heart 24:** heart problem, ex-partner, a dying love.
Coffin – **Ring 25:** widowhood.
Coffin – **Book 26:** Illness kept secret.
Coffin – **Letter 27:** announces a medical problem.
Coffin – **Mister 28:** a man in mourning or sick.
Coffin – **Lady 29:** a grieving or sick woman.
Coffin – **Lily 30:** lack of sexuality.
Coffin – **Sun 31:** healing.
Coffin – **Moon 32:** depression.
Coffin – **Key 33:** end of a misfortune, healing, a beneficial treatment.
Coffin – **Fish 34:** illness, bladder, kidneys.
Coffin – **Anchor 35:** incurable disease.
Coffin – **Cross 36:** very serious illness.

9- BOUQUET
QUEEN OF SPADE

MEANING OF THE CARD

The Bouquet represents joy, happiness and success. It is a token of protection and success. The Queen of Spades is a loving, fulfilled woman, single or widowed. The season is spring.

The Bouquet and other cards

Bouquet – Rider 1: happy visit.
Bouquet – Clover 2: luck, happiness, joy.
Bouquet – Ship 3: happy Journey.
Bouquet – House 4: happy home.
Bouquet – Tree 5: excellent health.
Bouquet – Cloud 6: happiness with small temporary worries.
Bouquet – Snake 7: happiness makes people envious.
Bouquet – Coffin 8: end of happiness.
Bouquet – Scythe 10: end of happiness because of an event.
Bouquet – Whip 11: happiness disturbed by quarrels.
Bouquet – Birds 12: happy conversation.

Bouquet – Child 13: happy child, swimming in happiness.
Bouquet – Fox 14: joy in work.
Bouquet – Bear 15: happy finance.
Bouquet – Star 16: serenity.
Bouquet – Stork 17: a change brings joy.
Bouquet – Dog 18: friend brings joy.
Bouquet – Haute Tour 19: happiness impossible to live.
Bouquet – Garden 20: happiness in the social circle, friendly.
Bouquet – Mount 21: obstacle to happiness.
Bouquet – Path 22: a choice leads to happiness.
Bouquet – Mouse 23: gloom.
Bouquet – Heart 24: romantic encounter filled with happiness.
Bouquet – Ring 25: a union swimming in happiness.
Bouquet – Book 26: secret Happiness.
Bouquet – Letter 27: happy news.
Bouquet – Mister 28: a happy man.
Bouquet – Lady 29: a happy woman.
Bouquet – Lily 30: happiness with righteousness, respect and honor.
Bouquet – Sun 31: divine happiness.
Bouquet – Moon 32: illusory happiness.
Bouquet – Key 33: opportunity for happiness to seize.
Bouquet – Fish 34: happiness in business.
Bouquet – Anchor 35: guaranteed, lasting happiness.
Bouquet – Cross 36: happiness destroyed by misfortune.

10- SCYTHE
JACK OF DIAMOND

MEANING OF THE CARD

The Scythe symbolizes a brutal, fast and difficult event such as an accident, an injury, a breakup. It represents urgency, the unexpected; cutting with one's past; making a decision. The jack of diamonds embodies a naive young man.

The Scythe and other cards

Scythe – Rider 1: the visitor will not come.
Scythe – Clover 2: end of lucky period.
Scythe – Ship 3: travel cancelled or unsafe.
Scythe – House 4: violence in the home.
Scythe – Tree 5: dental problem.
Scythe – Cloud 6: unforeseen change of short duration.
Scythe – Snake 7: breakup with hypocritical person.
Scythe – Coffin 8: accident or medical operation.
Scythe – Bouquet 9: sudden change towards happiness.
Scythe – Whip 11: physical quarrel.
Scythe – Birds 12: gossip about a separation.
Scythe – Child 13: abrupt change from

children or violent children.
Scythe – Fox 14: termination of employment contract.
Scythe – Bear 15: sudden loss of money.
Scythe – Star 16: decision to have serenity.
Scythe – Stork 17: rapid change expected.
Scythe – Dog 18: sudden friendly breakup.
Scythe – High Tower 19: administrative problem.
Scythe – Garden 20: social rupture.
Scythe – Mount 21: unexpected unpleasant event.
Scythe – Path 22: minor road accident.
Scythe – Mouse 23: unexpected expense.
Scythe – Heart 24: sudden emotional breakup.
Scythe – Ring 25: unexpected divorce.
Scythe – Book 26: a Secret revealed.
Scythe – Letter 27: announcement of a breakup by mail.
Scythe – Mister 28: sharp and brutal man.
Scythe – Lady 29: sharp and brutal woman.
Scythe – Lily 30: sudden change to be better.
Scythe – Sun 31: an excellent situation presents itself quickly.
Scythe – Moon 32: depression; breakup with a woman or illusions.
Scythe – Key 33: change after problem solving.
Scythe – Fish 34: stopping work as a self-employed person.
Scythe – Anchor 35: sudden change for a better situation.
Scythe - Cross 36: sorrow, misfortune comes by surprise.

11- WHIP
JACK OF CLUB

MEANING OF THE CARD

The Whip embodies physical violence, quarrels, turmoil, mistrust, the stroke of fate. Symbol of the phallus; muscles and tendons. The Jack of Clubs is an enterprising young brown-haired man. Period of two days; two weeks; two months.

The Whip and other cards

Whip – Rider 1: conflicting visitor.
Whip – Clover 2: luck in quarrels.
Whip – Ship 3: distance following conflict.
Whip – House 4: family dispute.
Whip – Tree 5: minor health problem.
Whip – Cloud 6: passing conflicts.
Whip – Snake 7: arguments, quarrels.
Whip – Coffin 8: poor health, pain.
Whip – Bouquet 9: sudden trouble.
Whip – Scythe 10: aggressive confit.
Whip – Birds 12: disputes, gossip.
Whip – Child 13: difficult child, who seeks conflicts.

Whip – **Fox 14:** quarrel at work.
Whip – **Bear 15:** financial conflicts.
Whip – **Star 16:** serenity found after arguments.
Whip – **Stork 17:** disagreement that creates changes.
Whip – **Dog 18:** argument with a friend.
Whip – **High Tower 19:** the courthouse.
Whip – **Garden 20:** conflicts with the social circle.
Whip – **Mount 21:** conflicts with powerful enemies.
Whip – **Path 22:** choice due to conflict.
Whip – **Mouse 23:** prolonged conflicts.
Whip – **Heart 24:** love disputes.
Whip – **Ring 25:** quarrels in the couple.
Whip – **Book 26:** conflicts kept secret.
Whip – **Letter 27:** bad news.
Whip – **Mister 28:** aggressive man.
Whip – **Lady 29:** aggressive woman.
Whip – **Lily 30:** distinguished man who only creates conflicts.
Verge – **Sun 31:** end of conflicts.
Verge – **Moon 32:** pain and sorrow.
Verge – **Key 33:** conflicts resolved.
Verge – **Fish 34:** conflict in independent work.
Verge – **Anchor 35:** Incessant arguments.
Whip – **Cross 36:** conflicts that cause suffering.

12- BIRDS
SEVEN OF DIAMOND

MEANING OF THE CARD

Associated with communication, the Birds announce chatter, talks, conflictual exchanges. The card represents a superficial, frivolous person. It symbolizes tension and nerves. Period of two months.

Birds and other cards

Birds – Rider 1: visitor who creates disputes.
Birds – Clover 2: excellent news.
Birds – Ship 3: discussion about a trip.
Birds – House 4: discussion about a house.
Birds – Tree 5: health undermined by tensions.
Birds – Cloud 6: passing quarrels.
Birds – Snake 7: lies.
Birds – Coffin 8: communication broken.
Birds – Bouquet 9: stormy conservation.
Birds – Scythe 10: discussion about a breakup.

Birds – **Whip 11:** violent dispute.
Birds – **Child 13:** dialogue with a child.
Birds – **Fox 14:** chatter at work.
Birds – **Bears 15:** financial discussion.
Birds – **Star 16:** serene conversation.
Birds – **Stork 17:** discussions about moving or a change.
Birds – **Dog 18:** discussion between friends.
Birds – **High Tower 19:** public communication or in a public place.
Birds – **Garden 20:** social success.
Birds – **Mount 21:** quarrel, dispute.
Birds – **Path 22:** exchanges to make a decision.
Birds – **Mouse 23:** exhausting discussion.
Birds – **Heart 24:** healthy dialogue in the couple.
Birds – **Ring 25:** couple who communicate a lot.
Birds – **Book 26:** secret discussion.
Birds – **Letter 27:** receiving a message.
Birds – **Mister 28:** a worried man.
Birds – **Lady 29:** a worried woman.
Birds – **Lily 30:** serene exchanges.
Birds – **Sun 31:** pleasant discussion.
Birds – **Moon 32:** lies.
Birds – **Key 33:** dialogue about a project.
Birds – **Fish 34:** independent business discussion.
Birds – **Anchor 35:** very deep tensions in the couple.
Birds – **Cross 36:** sad discussion that makes us unhappy.

13- CHILD
JACK OF PIQUE

MEANING OF THE CARD

The Child is a sign of vitality, renewal, joy of living, enthusiasm. It also represents youth and naivety; kindness. The Jack of Spades is a simple young man from the countryside. It is hope, the beginning.

The Child and the other cards

Child – Rider 1: arrival of a child.
Child – Clover 2: lucky child.
Child – Ship 3: naivety; journey of a child or a naive person.
Child – House 4: renewal in the home; child of the family.
Child – Tree 5: healthy child.
Child – Cloud 6: worried child or worries because of a child.
Child – Snake 7: hypocritical, lying child.
Child – Coffin 8: sick or deceased child.
Child – Bouquet 9: happy child.
Child – Scythe 10: abortion, miscarriage; angry child.

Child – Whip 11: child who creates disputes.
Child – Birds 12: discussion with children.
Child – Fox 14: contract for a young person or work with children.
Child – Bear 15: poor financial management for a child, a young person.
Child – Star 16: serene child.
Child – Stork 17: pregnancy, with the star she is going very well.
Child – Dog 18: childhood friend.
Child – High Tower 19: withdrawn child or young person or interned.
Child – Garden 20: group of young people, children.
Child – Mount 21: child blockage or big trouble because of a child.
Child – Path 22: choices to be made for a child.
Child – Mouse 23: child causes expenses.
Child – Heart 24: love of a child.
Child – Ring 25: arrival of a child in the couple.
Child – Book 26: student.
Child – Letter 27: news from a child.
Child – Mister 28: naive man.
Child – Lady 29: naive woman.
Child – Lily 30: distinguished and polite child.
Child – Sun 31: radiant child.
Child – Moon 32: depressed or moody child.
Child – Key 33: solution for a child.
Child – Fish 34: independent project.
Child – Anchor 35: attachment to youth; a childlike spirit, innocence.
Child – Cross 36: unhappy child or pregnancy at risk.

14- FOX
NINE OF CLOVER

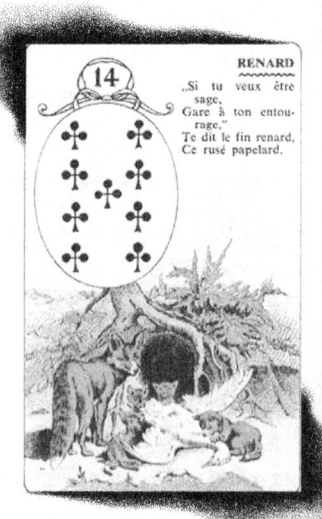

MEANING OF THE CARD

This is the card of work. The Fox embodies a cunning person to be wary of, a hypocrite who preserves his family. Avoid doing business with him. This is not the right time to act. The lungs, nose and ears are associated with it.

The Fox and other cards

Fox – Rider 1: visitor for work.
Fox – Clover 2: lucky professional environment.
Fox – Ship 3: business trip.
Fox – House 4: work at home.
Fox – Tree 5: work in the medical or paramedical field.
Fox – Cloud 6: temporary work.
Fox – Snake 7: hypocrisy in work.
Fox – Coffin 8: retreat; a job ends.
Fox – Bouquet 9: happy work.
Fox – Scythe 10: abrupt termination of an employment contract.
Fox – Whip 11: professional quarrels.

Fox – Birds 12: professional exchanges.
Fox – Child 13: apprenticeship contract or work with children, young people.
Fox – Bear 15: well-paid job.
Fox – Star 16: healthy professional environment.
Fox – Stork 17: change of job.
Fox – Dog 18: work with a friend.
Fox – High Tower 19: stable and reliable work.
Fox – Garden 20: professional ascension.
Fox – Mount 21: unemployment; professional blockage; boredom or isolation at work.
Fox – Path 22: professional choice.
Fox – Mouse 23: low-paid work.
Fox – Heart 24: love in the professional environment; passion for one's activity.
Fox – Ring 25: signing of an employment contract; professional association.
Fox – Book 26: administrative work; hidden work.
Fox – Letter 27: professional mail.
Fox – Mister 28: suspicious, cunning man.
Fox – Lady 29: suspicious, cunning woman.
Fox – Lily 30: peaceful work.
Fox – Sun 31: professional success.
Fox – Moon 32: boring work; professional illusion.
Fox – Key 33: professional opportunity.
Fox – Fish 34: self-employment.
Fox – Anchor 35: long-term contract.
Fox – Cross 36: loss of job.

15- BEAR
TEN OF CLOVER

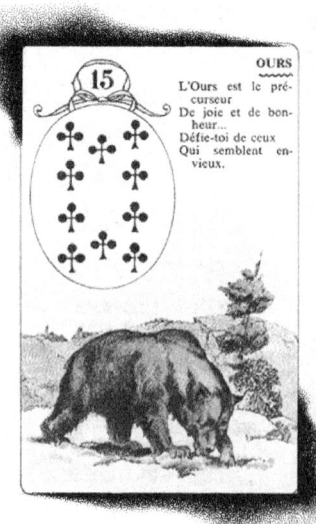

MEANING OF THE CARD

The Bear represents a strong and powerful person; a valuable support. This card symbolizes money, prosperous finances or crazy spending. It is a sign of longevity; a period of ten years.

The Bear and other cards

Bear – Knight 1: arrival of money.
Bear – Clover 2: unexpected cash inflow.
Bear – Ship 3: money gain from abroad or networks.
Bear – House 4: well-off home.
Bear – Tree 5: guaranteed money.
Bear – Cloud 6: temporary financial worries.
Bear – Snake 7: refund not executed.
Bear – Coffin 8: inheritance; donation.
Bear – Bouquet 9: happy finances.
Bear – Scythe 10: sudden sum spent.
Bear – Whip 11: financial quarrel.
Bear – Birds 12: financial discussion.

Bear – Child 13: financial naivety.
Bear – Fox 14: very well paid job.
Bear – Star 16: financial serenity.
Bear – Stork 17: financial change.
Bear – Dog 18: financial help from a friend.
Bear – High Tower 19: bank; taxes.
Bear – Garden 20: financial increase.
Bear – Mount 21: financial obstacle.
Bear – Path 22: financial choice.
Bear – Mouse 23: expenses to be expected.
Bear – Heart 24: connection between money and feelings.
Bear – Ring 25: financial association.
Bear – Book 26: hidden Money.
Bear – Letter 27: news regarding finances.
Bear – Mister 28: wealthy man.
Bear – Lady 29: wealthy woman.
Bear – Lily 30: money well placed
Bear – Sun 31: big money inflow; fortune.
Bear – Moon 32: financial illusion.
Bear – Key 33: solutions to financial problems.
Bear – Fish 34: job that brings in a lot of money.
Bear – Anchor 35: greed.
Bear – Cross 36: financial difficulties.

16- STAR
SIX OF HEART

MEANING OF THE CARD

The Star card is a sign of happiness, success, future improvement and hope. It represents the night; the skin and the face. The Star embodies a serene and courageous person.

The Star and other cards

Star – Rider 1: serene visitor.
Star – Clover 2: lucky break.
Star – Ship 3: serene vacation.
Star – House 4: serene home.
Star – Tree 5: excellent health.
Star – Cloud 6: temporary nervousness.
Star – Snake 7: false serenity or success.
Star – Coffin 8: end of nervousness, serene period arrives.
Star – Bouquet 9: joy, serenity.
Star – Scythe 10: serenity ends.
Star – Whip 11: quarrel about an improvement, an achievement.

Star – Birds 12: annoying dialogue.
Star – Child 13: serene child or youth.
Star – Fox 14: serene work.
Star – Bear 15: peaceful finances.
Star – Stork 17: serenity arrives.
Star – Dog 18: serene friend.
Star – High Tower 19: isolation to be serene; improvement with an institution.
Star – Garden 20: serene social relationship.
Star – Mount 21: obstacle to serenity.
Star – Path 22: serene choice, which leads to happiness, to improvement.
Star – Mouse 23: anxiety.
Star – Heart 24: serene love.
Star – Ring 25: successful, serene union.
Star – Book 26: moment of happiness kept secret.
Star – Letter 27: serene news.
Star – Mister 28: happy man.
Star – Lady 29: happy woman.
Star – Lily 30: serenity and pride.
Star – Sun 31: success and happiness.
Star – Moon 32: serenity and calm.
Star – Key 33: solution found to improve a situation; to obtain serenity.
Star – Fish 34: professional goal achieved.
Star – Anchor 35: loyalty.
Star – Cross 36: serenity spoiled by misfortune.

17- STORK
QUEEN OF HEART

MEANING OF THE CARD

The Stork indicates a change, a move. The Queen of Hearts is a blonde, gentle and loving woman, who is helpful. She also represents a mother, a birth, the gynecological parts; the present moment

The Stork and other cards

Stork – Rider 1: arrival of a mother, with the lily card is his own mother.
Stork – Clover 2: lucky change.
Stork – Ship 3: departure or change compared to abroad; with house moving abroad.
Stork – House 4: moving; with the map of the ship moving abroad.
Stork – Tree 5: healing.
Stork – Cloud 6: temporary worries due to of a change.
Stork – Snake 7: change that arouses jealousy and slander.
Stork – Coffin 8: gynecological problem.

Stork – Bouquet 9: change to a pleasant situation.
Stork – Scythe 10: breakup.
Stork – Whip 11: quarrel with a mother.
Stork – Birds 12: provocative Discussion changes.
Stork – Child 13: pregnancy; project.
Stork – Fox 14: change of job.
Stork – Bear 15: financial change.
Stork – Star 16: serene and happy change.
Stork – Dog 18: change of friend.
Stork – High Tower 19: isolation.
Stork – Garden 20: social change.
Stork – Mount 21: obstacle that causes changes.
Stork – Path 22: choices impose changes.
Stork – Mouse 23: change bothers, which causes losses.
Stork – Heart 24: change in love.
Stork – Ring 25: change in the couple.
Stork – Book 26: change kept secret.
Stork – Letter 27: news of change.
Stork – Mister 28: a changing man.
Stork – Lady 29: a changing woman.
Stork – Lily 30: the situation changes positively.
Stork – Sun 31: radiant change.
Stork – Moon 32: his mother or a mother.
Stork – Key 33: change brings the solution.
Stork – Fish 34: change in work.
Stork – Anchor 35: certain change.
Stork – Cross 36: change due to misfortune.

18- DOG
TEN OF HEART

MEANING OF THE CARD

A faithful, docile person, this card also represents friendship, friendly meetings, outings and invitations. The Dog symbolizes movement, language, as well as a long period.

The Dog and other cards

Dog – Rider 1: friendly visit.
Dog – Clover 2: lucky friend.
Dog – Ship 3: travel with a friend or a friend of foreign origin.
Dog – House 4: home of a friend.
Dog – Tree 5: faithful friend.
Dog – Cloud 6: temporary friendly tension.
Dog – Snake 7: hypocritical friend.
Dog – Coffin 8: death of a friend.
Dog – Bouquet 9: happy friendship.
Dog – Scythe 10: friendly breakup.
Dog – Whip 11: quarrel with a friend.
Dog – Birds 12: discussion between friends.

Dog – Child 13: naive friend.
Dog – Fox 14: work with a friend; work in a friendly atmosphere.
Dog – Bear 15: financial stability thanks to a friend.
Dog – Star 16: serenity among friends.
Dog – Stork 17: friendly changes.
Dog – High Tower 19: withdrawn, depressive friend.
Dog – Garden 20: circle of friends
Dog – Mount 21: friendship creates obstacles.
Dog – Path 22: friendly choice.
Dog – Mouse 23: friendship that deteriorates.
Dog – Heart 24: loving friendship.
Dog – Ring 25: united and faithful couple.
Dog – Book 26: a secret friend.
Dog – Letter 27: friendly news.
Dog – Mister 28: a man faithful in friendship.
Dog – Lady 29: woman faithful in friendship.
Dog – Lily 30: deep and sincere friendship.
Dog – Sun 31: radiant friend.
Dog – Moon 32: depressed friend.
Dog – Key 33: friend finds the solution.
Dog – Fish 34: friendly partners in business.
Dog – Anchor 35: strong friendship.
Dog – Cross 36: sad and unhappy friendship.

19- HIGH TOWER
SIX OF SPADE

MEANING OF THE CARD

The High Tower, symbol of stability and solidity, as well as isolation. It also represents an authority, an institution, an administration, a constructive event as well as the backbone.

The High Tower and other maps

High Tower – Rider 1: tax audit.
High Tower – Clover 2: administrative luck.
High Tower – Ship 3: solo travel.
High Tower – House 4: family isolation.
High Tower – Tree 5: very good health.
High Tower – Cloud 6: temporary worries with a public institution.
High Tower – Snake 7: brothel, site for adults; lonely deceitful person.
High Tower – Coffin 8: hospital.
High Tower – Bouquet 9: joy, well-being.
High Tower – Scythe 10: trouble with the law.
Haute Tour – Whip 11: tribunal.
High Tower – Birds 12: administrative discussion.

High Tower – Child 13: withdrawn, melancholic child or youth; juvenile facility.
High Tower – Fox 14: stable and safe work.
High Tower – Bear 15: bank.
High Tower – Star 16: serene evening.
High Tower – Stork 17: end of isolation; with the child's card is a maternity.
High Tower – Dog 18: loyal friendship.
High Tower – Garden 20: powerful social environment.
High Tower – Mount 21: administrative obstacle.
High Tower – Path 22: mandatory choice compared to to an administration.
High Tower – Mouse 23: isolation.
High Tower – Heart 24: solitude.
High Tower – Ring 25: strong and durable couple.
High Tower – Book 26: administrative papers undisclosed.
High Tower – Letter 27: news from the administration.
High Tower – Mister 28: lonely man.
High Tower – Lady 29: lonely woman.
High Tower – Lily 30: benevolent authority.
High Tower – Sun 31: recognized authority.
High Tower – Moon 32: psychiatric hospital, depression.
High Tower – Key 33: the administration brings a solution.
High Tower – Fish 34: doctor.
High Tower – Anchor 35: person who can be associated.
High Tower – Cross 36: great unfortunate person who causes depression.

20- GARDEN
EIGHT OF SPADE

MEANING OF THE CARD

The Garden represents an original, creative, tasteful and nature-loving person. Embodiment of social success and fame. This card is a sign of good health and a long period ahead.

The Garden and other maps

Garden – Rider 1: social ascension.
Garden – Clover 2: chance to seize.
Garden – Ship 3: foreign friends.
Garden – House 4: radiant fireplace.
Garden – Tree 5: healthy and balanced social circle.
Garden – Cloud 6: tensions with friends, within a social circle or with work colleagues.
Garden – Snake 7: jealous and envied situation.
Garden – Coffin 8: need to meditate, to distance oneself socially.
Garden – Bouquet 9: social ease.
Garden – Scythe 10: relationship breakdown.
Garden – Whip 11: argument with friends, work colleagues or a group of people.

Garden – **Birds 12:** lively discussion in the social circle.
Garden – **Child 13:** childishness.
Garden – **Fox 14:** professional recognition.
Garden – **Bear 15:** increase in finances.
Garden – **Star 16:** serene friendly circle.
Garden – **Stork 17:** social change; social promotion.
Garden – **Dog 18:** loyal friends.
Garden – **High Tower 19:** conciliatory administration.
Garden – **Mount 21:** rejection of friends, social circle.
Garden – **Path 22:** choices to be made in the social environment.
Garden – **Mouse 23:** excessive spending.
Garden – **Heart 24:** warm social circle.
Garden – **Ring 25:** friendly employment contract.
Garden – **Book 26:** celebrity.
Garden – **Letter 27:** recognition, talent, diploma.
Garden – **Mister 28:** radiant, original, creative, sociable man; friendly.
Garden – **Lady 29:** radiant, original, creative, sociable woman; friendly.
Garden – **Lys 30:** exceptional social circle.
Garden – **Sun 31:** fullness and social fulfillment.
Garden – **Moon 32:** friendly illusion.
Garden – **Key 33:** problem solved by the friendly circle.
Garden – **Fish 34:** promotion or professional fame.
Garden – **Anchor 35:** philanthropy.
Garden – **Cross 36:** misfortune, sadness in the social environment.

21- MONT
EIGHT OF CLOVER

MEANING OF THE CARD

The Mount foretells an obstacle, a stop, discouragement or a test to overcome. It can also be an enemy or a powerful ally depending on the cards that accompany it. The head is symbolized by the Mount.

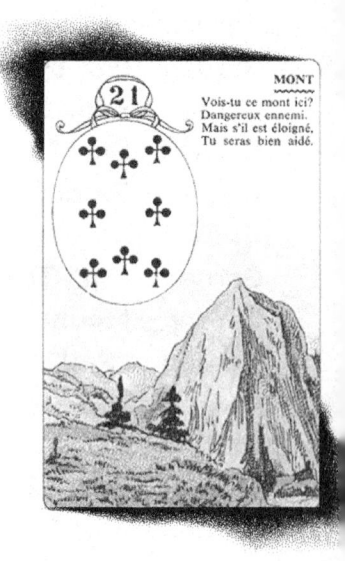

The Mount and other maps

Mount – Rider 1: a big problem is coming.
Mount – Clover 2: a big problem ends.
Mount – Ship 3: an obstacle that cancels a journey, a move; with a foreigner.
Mount – House 4: family worries.
Mountain – Tree 5: headaches.
Mount – Cloud 6: major temporary problem.
Mount – Snake 7: a hypocritical person creates trouble.
Mount – Coffin 8: serious illness.
Mount – Bouquet 9: solving a big problem.
Mount – Scythe 10: end of worries.
Mount – Whip 11: conflicts with an enemy.

Mount – Birds 12: dispute because of gossip.
Mont – Child 13: difficulties with a child.
Mont – Fox 14: unemployment, obstacle in work or because of a cunning person.
Mont – Ours 15: financial blockages.
Mount – Star 16: serenity in the face of obstacles.
Mont – Cigogne 17: change due to a major problem.
Mount – Dog 18: obstacle with a friend.
Mont – Haute Tour 19: administrative problems; isolation.
Mount – Garden 20: rejected by a social circle.
Mont – Path 22: when faced with a problem, a choice must be made.
Mount – Mouse 23: disputes.
Mount – Heart 24: emotional difficulty.
Mount – Ring 25: separation of a union.
Mount – Book 26: administrative obstacle; difficulties kept secret.
Mount – Letter 27: bad news.
Mont – Monsieur 28: a man with big blockages.
Mont – Dame 29: a woman with major blockages.
Mont – Lys 30: dignified in the face of worries.
Mont – Soleil 31: very important support.
Mount – Moon 32: significant psychiatric problem.
Mount – Key 33: solution to obstacles.
Mount – Pisces 34: professional problem; obstacle to abundance.
Mount – Anchor 35: lasting obstacle.
Mont-Croix 36: unhappy, sadness, mourning.

22- PATH
QUEEN OF DIAMONDS

MEANING OF THE CARD

The Path symbolizes choices; travel on the road; arteries and varicose veins. The Queen of Diamonds is energetic, gifted in communication and business. She may be of foreign origin. Period of six to seven weeks.

The Path and other maps

Path – Rider 1: visitor is on his way.
Path – Clover 2: good choice; lucky choice.
Path – Ship 3: distance.
Path – House 4: family choice.
Path – Tree 5: choices regarding health.
Path – Cloud 6: passing choices.
Path – Snake 7: bad choice.
Path – Coffin 8: vein problems.
Path – Bouquet 9: happy choice.
Path – False 10: minor road accident.
Path – Rod 11: choice causes argument.
Path – Birds 12: discussion regarding a choice.

Path – Child 13: choice in relation to a child.
Path – Fox 14: choice in work.
Path – Bear 15: financial choices.
Path – Star 16: choice of tranquility.
Path – Stork 17: a decision provokes a change.
Path – Dog 18: choice in the social circle.
Path – High Tower 19: administrative choice.
Path – Garden 20: choice between friends.
Path – Mount 21: very bad choice.
Path – Mouse 23: dispute following a choice.
Path – Heart 24: sentimental choice.
Path – Ring 25: choice in a couple, in a union.
Path – Book 26: choice over a secret.
Path – Letter 27: mail on the way.
Path – Mister 28: a man who must make a choice.
Path – Lady 29: a woman who has to make a choice.
Path – Lys 30: choice to preserve one's dignity.
Path – Sun 31: excellent choice.
Path – Moon 32: illusion regarding a choice.
Path – Key 33: choice that solves worries.
Path – Fish 34: choice in a self-employment.
Path – Anchor 35: a choice is imposed.
Path - Cross 36: a choice to be made, very painful.

23- MOUSE
SEVEN OF CLOVER

MEANING OF THE CARD

The Mouse card signifies loss, theft, greed, breach of trust; anxiety, something that eats away little by little. The seven of clubs represents someone manipulative, profiteering; waste of time.

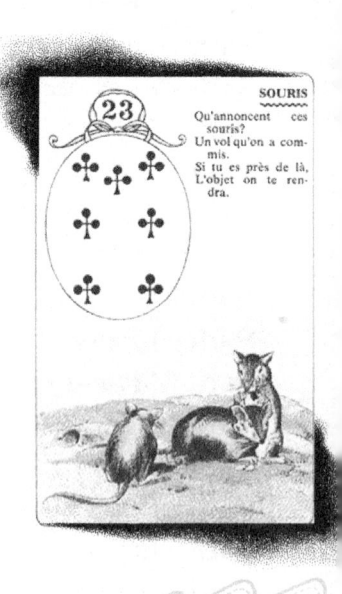

The Mouse and other cards

Mouse – **Rider 1:** visitor is late in arriving.
Mouse – **Clover 2:** luck comes slowly.
Mouse – **Ship 3:** travel cancelled.
Mouse – **House 4:** excessive spending on the home.
Mouse – **Tree 5:** minor health problem.
Mouse – **Cloud 6:** losses, passing quarrels.
Mouse – **Snake 7:** tensions because of a jealous and hypocritical person.
Mouse – **Coffin 8:** anxiety, gnawing illness; joint problems.
Mouse – **Bouquet 9:** happiness comes little by little.
Mouse – **Scythe 10:** problem due to an unexpected outflow of money.
Mouse – **Whip 11:** disputes, quarrels that gnaw away.

Mice – Birds 12: discussion that leads to conflict; waste of time.
Mouse – Child 13: anxious, annoying child.
Mouse – Fox 14: work that doesn't pay.
Mouse – Bear 15: very poor financial management.
Mouse – Star 16: serenity is slowly returning.
Mouse – Stork 17: a change that causes anxiety, brings worries, losses.
Mouse – Dog 18: boring friend.
Mouse – High Tower 19: isolation or bad thinking; administrative loss.
Mouse – Garden 20: unnecessary and harmful expenditure.
Mouse – Mount 21: big argument or loss.
Mouse – Path 22: choice that creates tension.
Mouse – Heart 24: decrease in feelings.
Mouse – Ring 25: a relationship or agreement is crumbling.
Mouse – Book 26: boring administrative papers; loss kept secret.
Mouse – Letter 27: invoices.
Mouse – Mister 28: poor and anxious man.
Mouse – Lady 29: poor and anxious woman.
Mouse – Lily 30: exhausting obligations.
Mouse – Sun 31: too many invitations; optimism is slowly returning.
Mouse – Moon 32: addiction.
Mouse – Key 33: problem of loss or anxiety resolved.
Mouse – Fish 34: self-employment brings no income and causes losses.
Mouse – Anchor 35: continual loss or quarrel.
Mouse – Cross 36: bankruptcy, total loss.

24- HEART
JACK OF HEART

MEANING OF THE CARD

The Heart symbolizes love. It also represents passion, happiness, complicity, harmony and the spring period. The Jack of Heart is a man, young, honorable, in love and combative.

The Heart and other cards

Heart – Rider 1: romantic visit.
Heart – Club 2: thunderbolt.
Heart – Ship 3: love abroad, far away or with a foreign person.
Heart – House 4: happy, warm home.
Heart – Tree 5: harmony, sincere feelings.
Heart – Cloud 6: temporary emotional difficulties.
Heart – Snake 7: infidelity, hypocrisy.
Heart – Coffin 8: ex-spouse; heart disease.
Heart – Bouquet 9: happy, perfect love.
Heart – Scythe 10: breakup.
Heart – Whip 11: love quarrel.
Heart – Bird 12: temporary infidelity; discussion related to feelings.

Heart – Child 13: love of a child; naive love.
Heart – Fox 14: deception in love; passion for his work; love at work.
Heart – Bear 15: financial abundance; feelings strong and powerful.
Heart – Star 16: serene feelings.
Heart – Stork 17: fleeting relationship, feelings which change.
Heart – Dog 18: friendly love; loving friend.
Heart – High Tower 19: stable, solid feelings.
Heart – Garden 20: warm social environment.
Heart – Mount 21: separation of a couple; obstacle to happiness.
Heart – Path 22: sentimental choice.
Heart – Mouse 23: feelings that crumble.
Heart – Ring 25: couple very much in love.
Heart – Book 26: secret relationship.
Heart – Letter 27: love letter.
Heart – Mister 28: spouse, lover; a happy man, in love.
Heart – Lady 29: spouse, lover; a happy woman, in love.
Heart – Lily 30: sincere love.
Heart – Sun 31: radiant love.
Heart – Moon 32: love illusion.
Heart – Key 33: love in perspective; sentimental solution.
Heart – Fish 34: love and work linked.
Heart – Anchor 35: lasting, sincere and deep love.
Heart – Cross 36: unhappy love.

25- RING
ACE OF CLOVER

MEANING OF THE CARD

The Ring is the symbol of a union, an agreement between one or more people. It is the start of a project. It also represents a precious object, chronic diseases. Period of seven years.

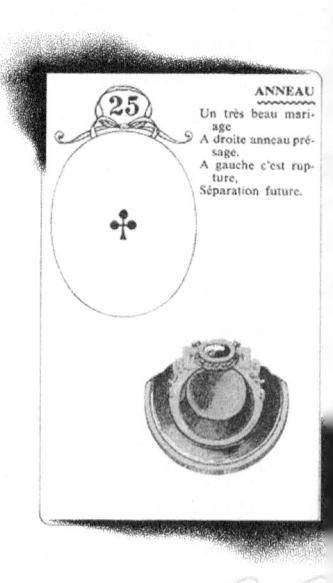

The Ring and other cards

Ring – Rider 1: arrival of a union.
Ring – Clover 2: luck and happiness in a couple; a lucky contract.
Ring – Ship 3: travel as a couple; contract or marriage with a foreign person.
Ring – House 4: real estate purchase.
Ring – Tree 5: healthy couple; contract in the health field.
Ring – Cloud 6: temporary worries in a union.
Ring – Snake 7: infidelity in the couple; lying or jealous contract or union.
Ring – Coffin 8: widowhood or end of something in the couple.
Ring – Bouquet 9: happy couple, in love.
Ring – Scythe 10: breakup or divorce.

Ring – Whip 11: dispute within a union.
Ring – Birds 12: discussion in the couple.
Ring – Child 13: arrival of a child, of a project.
Ring – Fox 14: signing employment contract.
Ring – Bear 15: financial contracts, credit.
Ring – Star 16: serene climate.
Ring – Stork 17: change in family or in a commitment.
Ring – Dog 18: faithful couple, very friendly; contract with a friend.
Ring – High Tower 19: stable and lasting union.
Ring – Garden 20: couple with many friends.
Ring – Mount 21: obstacle to a contract or which creates a separation in the couple.
Ring – Path 22: partner choice.
Ring – Mouse 23: couple or union that is crumbling.
Ring – Heart 24: harmonious and lasting union.
Ring – Book 26: secret relationship; contract kept secret; partnership with teaching.
Ring – Letter 27: news from the partner.
Ring – Mister 28: a married man, spouse.
Ring – Lady 29: a married woman, spouse.
Ring – Lily 30: stable and lasting relationship.
Ring – Sun 31: fulfilled marriage; happy contract.
Ring – Moon 32: austere relationship.
Ring – Key 33: couple forming; solution to a contract.
Ring – Fish 34: professional association.
Ring – Anchor 35: faithful couple, stable union.
Ring – Cross 36: heartache, unhappy union.

26- BOOK
TEN OF DIAMOND

MEANING OF THE CARD

The Book represents knowledge, intelligence, studies, exams, administrative documents but also secrets. The unconscious is also symbolized by this card, as well as esotericism.

The Book and other cards

Book – Rider 1: secret revealed by a visitor.
Book – Clover 2: good news.
Book – Ship 3: travel or movement kept secret; schooling, exam abroad.
Book – House 4: family secret.
Book – Tree 5: healthy situation.
Book – Cloud 6: annoying situation; short-term training.
Book – Snake 7: secret revealed.
Book – Coffin 8: latent disease.
Book – Bouquet 9: happy situation or study.
Book – Scythe 10: sudden cessation of studies; secret revealed.
Book – Whip 11: a secret that causes anger, quarrels.

Book – Birds 12: discussion kept secret or concerning studies.
Book – Child 13: student; secret concerning a child.
Book – Fox 14: employ; concealed work.
Book – Bear 15: secret money.
Book – Star 16: serene situation.
Book – Stork 17: change of situation.
Book – Dog 18: secret friendship.
Book – High Tower 19: administration, institution.
Book – Garden 20: celebrity, fame.
Book – Mount 21: obstacle or secret that blocks.
Book – Path 22: forced choice because of a revealed secret or related to studies.
Book – Mouse 23: secret that undermines, that gnaws.
Book – Heart 24: hidden feelings of love.
Book – Ring 25: secret relationship or union.
Book – Letter 27: administrative papers.
Book – Mister 28: a secretive man; intelligent; a teacher.
Book – Lady 29: a secretive woman; intelligent; a teacher.
Book – Lily 30: noble secret; study of law.
Book – Sun 31: secret revealed that pleases.
Book – Moon 32: study of the unconscious, esotericism.
Book – Key 33: secret element that provides a solution; hidden solution.
Book – Fish 34: intellectual work, writer, independent trainer.
Book – Anchor 35: well-kept secret.
Book – Cross 36: secret that makes you unhappy.

27- LETTER
SEVEN OF SPADE

MEANING OF THE CARD

The Letter symbolizes a mail, news; a writer; a sociable person, eager to learn, curious. It is also the sign of a passing feeling. Time is fast.

The Letter and other cards

Letter – Rider 1: a visitor arrives quickly.
Letter – Clover 2: good news.
Letter – Ship 3: news from abroad.
Letter – House 4: family news.
Letter – Tree 5: healing.
Letter – Cloud 6: temporary bad news.
Letter – Snake 7: betrayal; lying news.
Letter – Coffin 8: announcement of a death; of the end of something.
Letter – Bouquet 9: excellent news.
Letter – Scythe 10: breakup letter.
Letter – Whip 11: conflicting news, aggressive mail.

Letter – Birds 12: e-mail, SMS, social networks.
Letter – Child 13: news from a child, from a young person.
Letter – Fox 14: news of a job, of an activity.
Letter – Bear 15: financial news.
Letter – Star 16: serene news.
Letter – Stork 17: news that brings changes.
Letter – Dog 18: friendly news.
Letter – High Tower 19: mail or administrative paper.
Letter – Garden 20: good administrative, institutional news.
Letter – Mount 21: bad news; obstacle.
Letter – Path 22: news that arrives or that allows to make a choice.
Letter – Mouse 23: invoices.
Letter – Heart 24: love letter.
Letter – Ring 25: business contract, marriage contract.
Letter – Book 26: announcement of a secret.
Letter – Mister 28: a man who receives news.
Letter – Lady 29: a woman receiving news.
Letter – Lys 30: good news from a man.
Letter – Sun 31: excellent news.
Letter – Moon 32: imaginary story, dream.
Letter – Key 33: news that solves a problem.
Letter – Fish 34: news concerning independent professions; abundance.
Letter – Anchor 35: confirmation of upcoming news.
Letter – Cross 36: unfortunate and sad news.

28- MISTER
ACE OF HEART

MEANING OF THE CARD

The Mister embodies the consultant or an important man in our life such as the husband, a friend, a father. The ace of hearts is a sign of joy and love.

The Mister and the other cards

Mister – Rider 1: arrival of a man.
Mister – Clover 2: a lucky man.
Mister – Ship 3: a man abroad; who likes to escape or who has to move.
Mister – House 4: a generous, healthy man.
Mister – Tree 5: a healthy and balanced man.
Mister – Cloud 6: temporary torment for a man or the consultant.
Mister – Snake 7: a fickle man; hypocrite to be wary of; betrayal.
Mister – Coffin 8: a grieving or sick man.
Mister – Bouquet 9: blossoming union.
Mister – Scythe 10: a violent man.
Mister – Whip 11: a quarrelsome man.

Mister – Birds 12: a worried man.
Mister – Child 13: a naive, immature man.
Mister – Fox 14: a cunning, suspicious man.
Mister - Bear 15: a man with a stable and lasting financial situation; a protector.
Mister – Star 16: a serene man.
Mister – Stork 17: a man with a changeable mood; with the House a move.
Mister – Dog 18: a man loyal in friendship.
Mister – High Tower 19: a lonely man.
Mister – Garden 20: a socially fulfilled man.
Mister – Mont 21: a man facing major problems.
Mister – Path 22: a man must make a choice.
Mister – Mouse 23: a man suffers losses.
Mister – Heart 24: a warm, loving man.
Mister – Ring 25: a married man.
Mister – Book 26: a secretive Man.
Mister – Letter 27: a man is going to receive news or news of a man.
Mister – Lady 29: a couple.
Mister – Lys 30: a man of integrity.
Mister – Sun 31: a warm man.
Mister – Moon 32: a dreamy, moody, depressive man.
Mister – Key 33: one man has the solution.
Mister – Fish 34: a creative man.
Mister – Anchor 35: a man has a deep attachment.
Mister – Cross 36: an unhappy man, who undergoes trials.

29- LADY
ACE OF SPADE

MEANING OF THE CARD

The Lady embodies the consultant. She can also represent the wife, a friend, a mother. The Ace of Spade announces success; perseverance in the face of adversity.

The Lady and the other cards

Lady – Rider 1: arrival of a woman.
Lady – Clover 2: a lucky woman.
Lady – Ship 3: a woman abroad; who likes to escape or who has to move.
Lady – House 4: a generous woman.
Lady – Tree 5: a generous, balanced woman.
Lady – Cloud 6: temporary torment for a woman or the consultant.
Lady – Snake 7: a fickle woman; dishonest to be wary of; betrayal.
Lady – Coffin 8: a grieving or sick woman.
Lady – Bouquet 9: blossoming union.
Lady – Scythe 10: a violent woman.
Lady – Whip 11: a quarrelsome woman.

Lady – Birds 12: a troubled woman.
Lady – Child 13: a naive, immature woman.
Lady – Fox 14: a cunning, suspicious woman.
Lady – Bear 15: a woman with a stable and lasting financial situation; a protector.
Lady – Star 16: a serene woman.
Lady – Stork 17: a moody woman; with moving house.
Lady – Dog 18: a woman faithful in friendship.
Lady – High Tower 19: a lonely woman.
Lady – Garden 20: a woman fulfilled in a social circle.
Lady – Mount 21: a woman facing a major problem.
Lady – Path 22: a woman must make a choice.
Lady – Mouse 23: a woman suffers losses.
Lady – Heart 24: a warm woman.
Lady – Ring 25: a married woman.
Lady – Book 26: a secret woman.
Lady – Letter 27: a woman is going to receive news or news from a woman.
Lady – Mister 28: a married woman.
Lady – Lily 30: a woman of integrity and trust.
Lady – Sun 31: a warm, radiant woman.
Lady – Moon 32: a dreamy, moody, depressive woman.
Lady – Key 33: a woman has the solution.
Lady – Fish 34: woman with a creative profession.
Lady – Anchor 35: a woman has a deep attachment.
Lady – Cross 36: an unhappy woman, who undergoes trials.

30- LILY
KING OF SPADE

MEANING OF THE CARD

The Lily symbolizes righteousness, nobility, loyalty and sincerity. Predicts a pure heart or future happiness. The King of Spade embodies a good, protective man, a man of law. The period is winter.

The Lily and other cards

Lily – Rider 1: upright and loyal visitor.
Lily – Clover 2: luck coming from a devoted person; gratification.
Lily – Ship 3: help from a person of foreign origin; sincerity creates a distance.
Lily – House 4: home filled with goodness.
Lily – Tree 5: serenity and loyalty.
Lily – Cloud 6: temporary difficulty related to the law.
Lily – Snake 7: lies; lack of trust.
Lily – Coffin 8: serene period that is ending.
Lily – Bouquet 9: divine happiness.
Lily – Scythe 10: sexual assault; theft, scam.
Lily – Whip 11: righteousness that leads to combat.
Lily – Birds 12: joyful and serene discussion.

Lily – Child 13: serious and honest child or young person; modesty, humility.
Lily – Fox 14: honesty and uprightness in the professional environment.
Lily – Bear 15: financial stability.
Lily – Star 16: dignity, serenity; purity.
Lily – Stork 17: stability.
Lily – Dog 18: sincere and loyal friend.
Lily – High Tower 19: a representative of the law; administrative uprightness; a loyal, solitary man.
Lily – Garden 20: noble social circle; social pride and happiness.
Lily – Mount 21: obstacle to be feared.
Lily – Path 22: honesty and uprightness demand to choose.
Lily – Mouse 23: need rest.
Lily – Heart 24: sincere love.
Lily – Ring 25: serene and upright union.
Lily – Book 26: respect, simplicity; legal procedures.
Lily – Letter 27: serene friendly mail; loyal contract.
Lily – Mister 28: an honest and peaceful man.
Lily – Lady 29: an honest and peaceful woman.
Lily – Sun 31: a radiant, sincere, noble and venerable man; joy.
Lily – Moon 32: a worthy, sincere, noble and venerable woman; nostalgia.
Lily – Key 33: deal done.
Lily – Fish 34: bourgeoisie; happiness in business.
Lily – Anchor 35: dignity; lasting loyalty.
Lily – Croix 36: chagrin.

31- SUN
ACE OF DIAMOND

MEANING OF THE CARD

The Sun embodies the masculine. It symbolizes radiance, optimism, prosperity, as well as the summer season. The Ace of Diamond announces success in all areas, joy, luck, fame and celebrity.

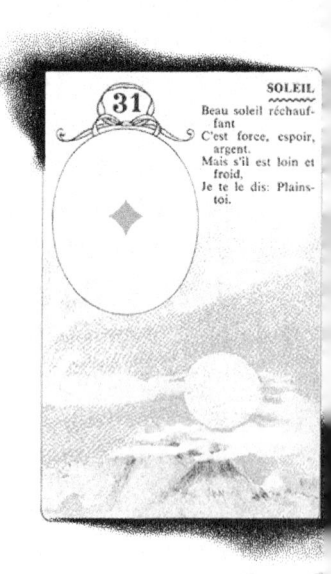

The Sun and other cards

Sun – Rider 1: arrival of a lucky visitor.
Sun – Clover 2: lots of luck.
Sun – Ship 3: holidays in the sun.
Sun – House 4: family happiness.
Sun – Tree 5: joy, health, prosperity.
Sun – Cloud 6: small temporary problem.
Sun – Snake 7: jealous of his success.
Sun – Coffin 8: happiness ends.
Sun – Bouquet 9: great happiness.
Sun – Scythe 10: happiness broken by an upheaval.
Sun – Whip 11: happiness spoiled by quarrels.
Sun – Birds 12: radiant discussion.

Sun – Child 13: happy child.
Sun – Fox 14: professional success.
Sun – Bear 15: wealth.
Sun – Star 16: perfect happiness.
Sun – Stork 17: success has arrived.
Sun – Dog 18: radiant friend.
Sun – High Tower 19: literary success.
Sun – Garden 20: warm social circle.
Sun – Mount 21: big worry.
Sun – Path 22: all paths lead to success.
Sun – Mouse 23: successes spoiled by small worries.
Sun – Heart 24: radiant love.
Sun – Ring 25: warm union.
Sun – Book 26: secret happiness.
Sun – Letter 27: excellent news.
Sun – Mister 28: radiant man.
Sun – Lady 29: radiant woman.
Sun – Lily 30: nobility, righteousness.
Sun – Moon 32: perfect agreement.
Sun – Key 33: assured success.
Sun – Fish 34: success in an independent profession.
Sun – Anchor 35: success continues.
Sun – Cross 36: success spoiled by misfortune.

32- MOON
EIGHT OF HEART

MEANING OF THE CARD

The Moon embodies the feminine. It symbolizes the night, the occult, spirituality, the unconscious, dreams and the imaginary. Moody, melancholic, cold people are represented by this card.

The Moon and other cards

Moon – Rider 1: visit or message from a woman, with the stork it is his mother.
Moon – Clover 2: luck comes after a period of trouble.
Moon – Ship 3: illusion regarding a journey.
Moon – House 4: family worries.
Moon – Tree 5: hypochondriac person.
Moon – Cloud 6: temporary mental disorder.
Moon – Snake 7: illusion, hypocrisy coming from a woman, a mother or a moody, cold person.
Moon – Coffin 8: depression.
Moon – Bouquet 9: wandering.
Moon – Scythe 10: end of illusions.

Moon – Whip 11: sorrow, sadness.
Moon – Birds 12: lies, broken promises.
Moon – Child 13: moody child or child with psychiatric disorders.
Moon – Fox 14: professional illusion.
Moon – Bear 15: financial illusion.
Moon – Star 16: serene night or evening.
Moon – Stork 17: his mother.
Moon – Dog 18: friendly deception or melancholy friend.
Moon – High Tower 19: isolation, depression.
Moon – Garden 20: utopian social circle.
Moon – Mount 21: psychiatric disorder.
Moon – Path 22: choice to be made following confusion.
Moon – Mouse 23: psychological problem, anxiety.
Moon – Heart 24: feeling cold and distant.
Moon – Ring 25: icy or illusory union.
Moon – Book 26: secret garden, the occult, spirituality.
Moon – Letter 27: long-awaited news.
Moon – Mister 28: a moody, depressive man.
Moon – Lady 29: a moody, depressive woman.
Moon – Lily 30: grief dissipates.
Moon – Sun 31: perfect harmony between a woman and a man.
Moon – Key 33: long solution to find.
Moon – Fish 34: illusion in an independent profession or imaginary abundance.
Moon – Anchor 35: deep psychiatric disorder.
Moon – Cross 36: much sorrow.

33- KEY
EIGHT OF DIAMOND

MEANING OF THE CARD

The Key opens new doors. It marks a new beginning and allows you to find solutions. The card announces success, achievement in all areas.

The Key and the other cards

Key – Rider 1: visitor brings the solution.
Key – Clover 2: problem solved by one move lucky.
Key – Ship 3: a journey will be made without worry.
Key – House 4: peaceful home, solution concerning a house.
Key – Tree 5: healing.
Key – Cloud 6: issue resolved.
Key – Snake 7: no harmful person reaches us.
Key – Coffin 8: disease treated with new treatment.
Key – Bouquet 9: happiness, success.
Key – Scythe 10: change for the better.
Key – Whip 11: solution found to conflicts.

Key – Birds 12: solution found following a discussion.
Key – Child 13: solution found for a child.
Key – Fox 14: professional opportunity.
Key – Bear 15: solution to financial problems.
Key – Star 16: peace of mind thanks to a solution.
Key – Stork 17: the solution arrives following a change.
Key – Dog 18: a friend brings the solution.
Key – High Tower 19: administration resolves a problem.
Key – Garden 20: solution found by the social circle.
Key – Mount 21: solution delayed by a major problem.
Key – Path 22: good choice.
Key – Mouse 23: solution is slowly coming.
Key – Heart 24: sentimental solution.
Key – Ring 25: solution to a union.
Key – Book 26: problem solved by learning or kept secret.
Key – Letter 27: problem solved thanks to a letter, a message.
Key – Mister 28: one man holds the solution.
Key – Lady 29: a woman holds the solution.
Key – Lily 30: problem solved with righteousness and dignity or by a person of law.
Key – Sun 31: no problems ahead.
Key – Moon 32: hidden and long solution to find.
Key – Fish 34: good business, abundance.
Key – Anchor 35: the solution has always been there.
Key – Cross 36: end of misfortune, of sorrow.

34- FISH
KING OF DIAMOND

MEANING OF THE CARD

The King of Diamond is an authoritarian, creative character, an entrepreneur. Pisces symbolizes abundance, financial success, an independent profession; the kidneys and the bladder.

Fish and other cards

Fish – Rider 1: professional visit.
Fish – Clover 2: excellent opportunity.
Fish – Ship 3: business travel.
Fish – House 4: owner, promoter, real estate agent.
Fish – Tree 5: professional project; healthy activity.
Fish – Cloud 6: temporary professional worries.
Fish – Snake 7: professional partner whose you have to be careful, not serious.
Fish – Coffin 8: retirement, end of an activity.
Fish – Bouquet 9: happiness in work.
Fish – Scythe 10: breach of contract.
Fish – whip 11: professional conflict.

Fish – Birds 12: discussion about an activity, a project, finances; lawyer.
Fish – Child 13: apprenticeship; first job; activity with Fish or young people.
Fish – Fox 14: liberal activity, commerce; beware of a person who is cunning in business.
Fish – Bear 15: money coming in through work.
Fish – Star 16: serene work.
Fish – Stork 17: professional change.
Fish – Dog 18: work with friends.
Fish – High Tower 19: doctor.
Fish – Garden 20: social ascension.
Fish – Mount 21: obstacle to abundance.
Fish – Path 22: a choice causes a change of direction.
Fish – Mouse 23: flight.
Fish – Heart 24: love and work related.
Fish – Ring 25: professional association.
Fish – Book 26: administrative work; writer, teacher, trainer.
Fish – Letter 27: professional news.
Fish – Mister 28: an enterprising man.
Fish – Lady 29: an enterprising woman.
Fish – Lily 30: bourgeoisie, high position.
Fish – Sun 31: radiant profession.
Fish – Moon 32: professional illusion.
Fish – Key 33: signed contract, solution to professional problems.
Fish – Anchor 35: work assured.
Fish – Cross 36: a job is not completed.

35- ANCHOR
NINE OF SPADE

MEANING OF THE CARD

The Anchor represents a deep attachment. Depending on the card that accompanies it, it indicates security, stability or a well-anchored blockage. Symbol of the pelvis and hips. Period that lasts.

The Anchor and other cards

Anchor – Rider 1: a friend arrives.
Anchor – Clover 2: success, luck.
Anchor – Ship 3: we find its home port.
Anchor – House 4: family attachment, to one's home.
Anchor – Tree 5: hypochondriac.
Anchor – Cloud 6: jealousy, worry about loyalty.
Anchor – Snake 7: success desire.
Anchor – Coffin 8: incurable disease.
Anchor – Bouquet 9: assurance of happiness.
Anchor – Scythe 10: instability.
Anchor – Whip 11: conflicts.

Anchor – Birds 12: disputes over fidelity.
Anchor – Child 13: child or young person with complexes.
Anchor – Fox 14: long-term, stable work.
Anchor – Bear 15: financial stability, greed.
Anchor – Star 16: lasting serenity; hope for success.
Anchor – Stork 17: change assured.
Anchor – Dog 18: loyal, long-time friend.
Anchor – High Tower 19: necessary isolation that lasts, lonely person.
Anchor – Garden 20: philanthropist.
Anchor – Mount 21: insurmountable obstacle.
Anchor – Path 22: imposing a choice.
Anchor – Mouse 23: financial imbalance.
Anchor – Heart 24: faithful and lasting feeling.
Anchor – Ring 25: stable union.
Anchor – Book 26: well-kept secret.
Anchor – Letter 27: assured news.
Anchor – Mister 28: a stable man.
Anchor – Lady 29: a stable woman.
Anchor – Lily 30: nobility, bourgeoisie.
Anchor – Sun 31: immense success.
Anchor – Moon 32: serious psychiatric disorder.
Anchor – Key 33: assurance of success.
Anchor – Fish 34: stable work if vocation.
Anchor – Cross 36: very great misfortune.

36- CROSS
SIX OF CLOVER

MEANING OF THE CARD

The Cross announces misfortune and pain. It represents a sad, pessimistic, tormented person. The taste for freedom, the occult, faith and the lower back are symbolized by the Cross. Period of two weeks.

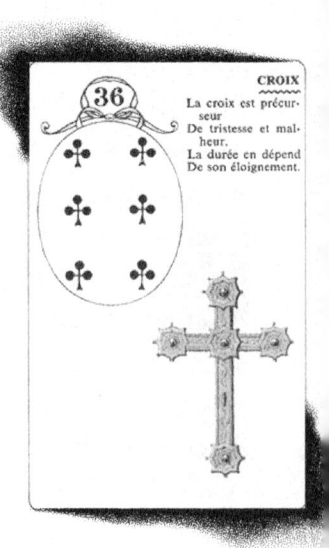

The Cross and other cards

Cross – Rider 1: bad news arrives.
Cross – Clover 2: luck ends sorrow.
Cross – Ship 3: sad and unhappy journey.
Cross – House 4: misfortune in the home.
Cross – Tree 5: misfortune in health.
Cross – Cloud 6: misfortune, temporary sadness.
Cross – Snake 7: jealous person who rejoices of our misfortune.
Cross – Coffin 8: serious and painful illness; death.
Cross – Bouquet 9: pleasant surprise in misfortune.
Cross – Scythe 10: end of misfortune, of sorrow.

Cross – Whip 11: dispute that causes sorrow.
Cross – Birds 12: unhappy discussion.
Cross – Child 13: sad child or young person.
Cross – Fox 14: a job will not be done; painful activity.
Cross – Bear 15: financial misfortune.
Cross – Star 16: serenity broken by misfortune.
Cross – Stork 17: change due to misfortune.
Cross – Dog 18: unhappy friend who bores us.
Cross – High Tower 19: church or religious monument.
Cross – Garden 20: social sadness.
Cross – Mount 21: misfortune difficult to overcome.
Cross – Path 22: unfortunate and difficult choice that is imposed.
Cross – Mouse 23: big money worries.
Cross – Heart 24: heartache.
Cross – Ring 25: unhappy union.
Cross – Book 26: religious.
Cross – Letter 27: unfortunate news.
Cross – Mister 28: a sad man.
Cross – Lady 29: a sad woman.
Cross – Lily 30: dignity in sorrow.
Cross – Sun 31: miracle.
Cross – Moon 32: melancholy, sorrow, depression.
Cross – Key 33: a solution to unhappiness brings joy.
Cross – Fish 34: error in work due to misfortune.
Cross – Anchor 35: assurance of misfortune.

PART TWO

READING MODELS

ONLINE READING

The online reading is the simplest. After shuffling the deck of cards, spread the cards face down, ask a question and draw a card while thinking about the situation. You can also try to visualize it.

The card turned over will give you a first interpretation. If this seems too vague and needs to be clarified, you can draw a second and a third if necessary.

Let yourself be inspired by the images, trust your feelings and to help you, refer to the meanings of each card and their combinations.

Here is an example: Jeanne asks the question
Will I find a job within two months?

INTERPRETATION

The Birds indicate discussions regarding her job search, as well as a two-month period. In order to clarify the answer, Jeanne draws another card.

By associating it with the Garden card, discussions in her social circle will allow her to guide her research. She wants to refine the interpretation and draws another card.

The Lily symbolizes happiness and righteousness. Associated with the other cards, Jeanne has a good chance of finding a job that she will like in the coming months thanks to her social circle.

CROSS READING

The cross draw allows you to obtain an in-depth answer and make a decision when you are hesitant about a person or a situation.

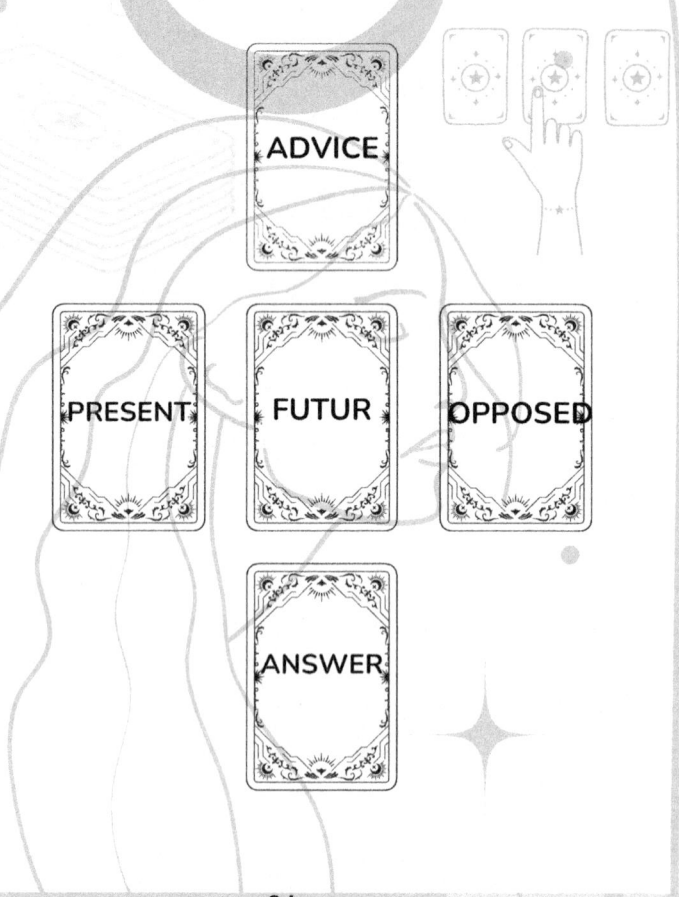

ADVICE

PRESENT FUTUR OPPOSED

ANSWER

COLUMN READING

This reading can be useful in the sentimental or relational field. Each column represents a person: romantic partners, work colleagues or family members.

Choose a card for each question asked by each person and place them on the same line.

For example: Which card represents the feelings each person has for the other?
What are they to each other?
What do they each want for the other?
How do they project themselves?

Person 1	Person 2
ANSWER	ANSWER

TRIANGLE READING

This is useful when you want to make a change in your life, such as in the professional field. This way you can weigh the pros and cons before making a decision.

For example: What will happen if I change jobs or stay in the current situation?

- Current State of Mind
- Advice for Change
- Advice for Staying
- Evolution with Change
- Evolution without Change

GLOBAL READING

This is an overview. Each card answers an area of your life. You can add a card on the folds of which you want more precision.

Current State of Mind	Challenge	Strength
Professional	Finance	Love
Advice	Evolution Futur	

INTUITIVE READING

This is a nine-card spread. Whether you have a specific area in mind or want to receive a message, the central card determines the Subject of your reading. Let your intuition guide you by observing the cards surrounding it and interpret them.

The position of the cards allows you to refine your reading and complete your messages, either vertically, horizontally or diagonally. The scan from left to right indicates the past, present and future.

In the case of a draw with a specific subject, place the card that represents the domain, for example the Dog for the friendly domain or the Fox for what concerns work as an employee. You can associate each card with that of the Subject, as well as with those that surround it.

LARGE READING BOARD

Create your own board from the 36 houses. They represent the 36 cards of the Petit LENORMAND. On each card is written their meanings by house. This explanatory table facilitates the learning of the game and helps you in reading the interpretations of the Large Reading Board LENORMAND.

1	2	3	4	5	6	7	8	9
10	11	12	13	14	15	16	17	18
19	20	21	22	23	24	25	26	27
28	29	30	31	32	33	34	35	36

Cut out the cards below and stick them on a large sheet of paper measuring at least 65 cm x 43 cm. Arrange them in 9 columns and 4 rows as shown above. This way, your reading board will allow you to make a complete draw relating to all areas of your life.

Once your table is complete, carry out your draw by covering all the houses with your 36 cards from the Petit LENORMAND game. Then turn the cards over and discover the message that corresponds to each house.

The reading is done from the consultant's card. Then start the interpretation in relation to the house where it is located. For example, the Lady is in the house of the Moon. Thus, you discover the general state of the consultant. Then you look for in which house the Moon is located and you continue in this way the reading for all the cards, so as to create the thread of the consultant's story.

Also pay attention to the position of the cards on the board. For example, whether the characters are looking at each other or not, whether they are looking towards the past or the future, which area their gaze is focused on.

You can also look at the cards that surround each area of life. For example, love life is represented by the Heart card. Look at which house it is located in. In this case, it is the Scythe, so there is something to decide. Then look at the cards that surround it to enlighten you and provide you with details on the evolution of the situation.

House 1
RIDER

News Messages Visitor Joints

Speed

House 2
CLOVER

Luck Happiness Success General Condition

1 to 6 weeks

House 3
SHIP

Travel Liver, Spleen

Speed

House 4
HOUSE

Hearth Family Prosperity Security

Longevity

House 5
TREE

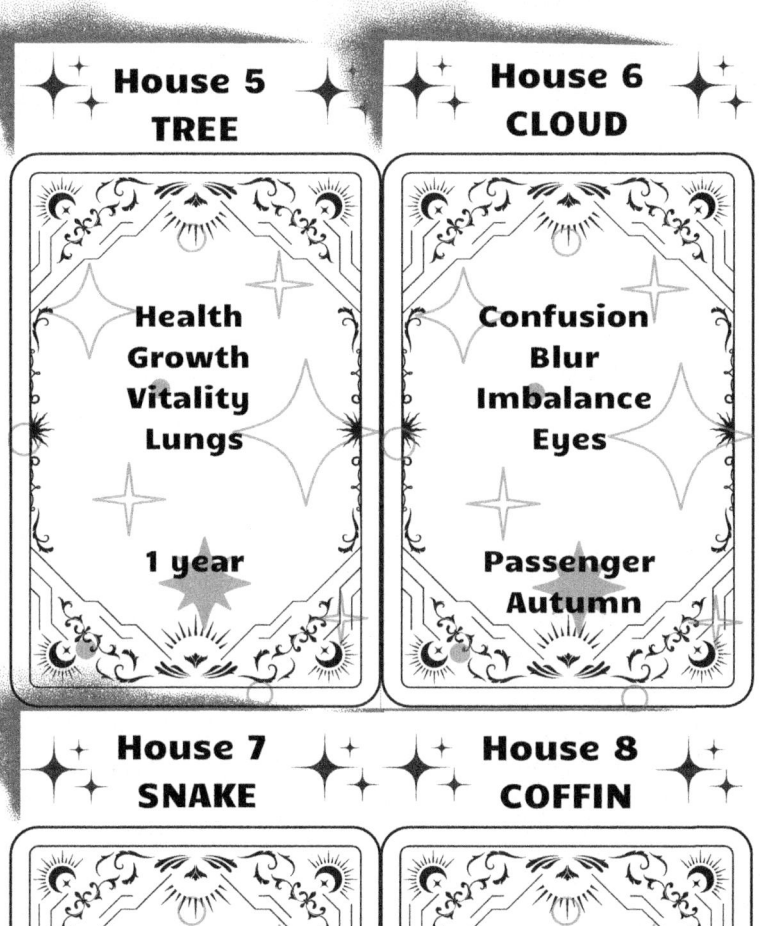

Health
Growth
Vitality
Lungs

1 year

House 6
CLOUD

Confusion
Blur
Imbalance
Eyes

Passenger
Autumn

House 7
SNAKE

Danger
Hypocrisy
Treachery
Intestines

Waiting

House 8
COFFIN

Grief
End
Transformation

Infinity

Maison 9 — BOUQUET

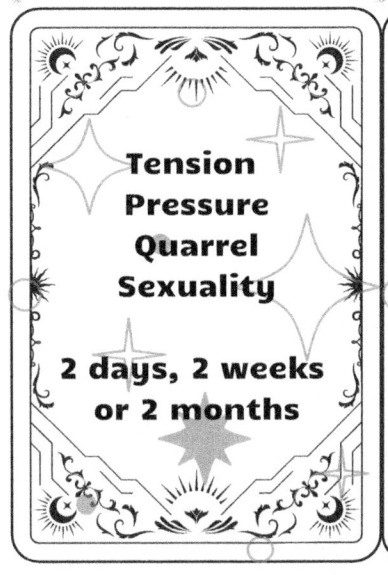

Joy, Happiness, Fulfillment, Success, Protection

Spring

House 10 — SCYTHE

Unexpected Cutoff Breakup

Fast

House 11 — WHIP

Tension
Pressure
Quarrel
Sexuality

2 days, 2 weeks or 2 months

House 12 — BIRDS

Chatter
Gossip
Discussion
Nervousness

2 months

House 13
CHILD

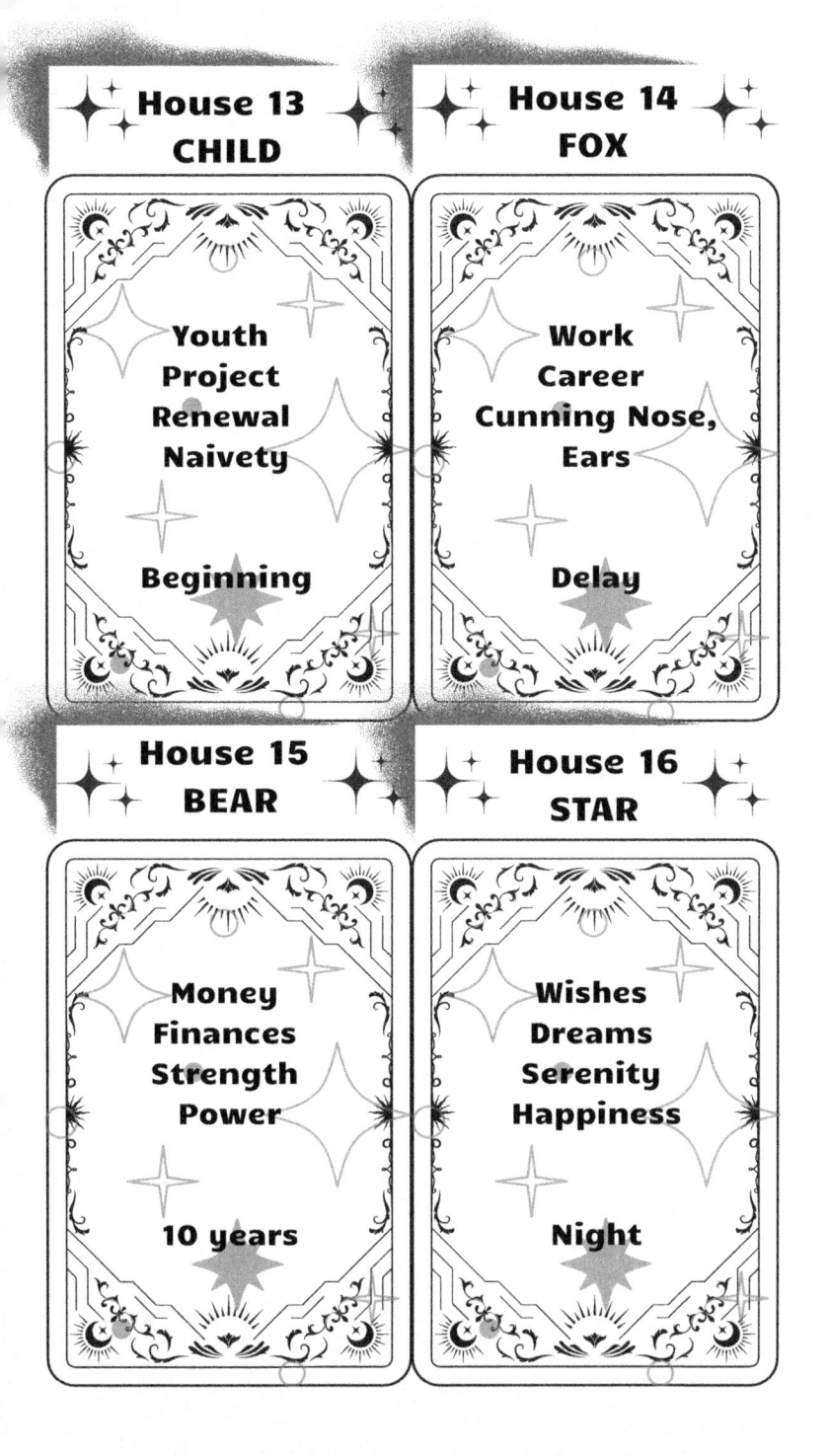

Youth
Project
Renewal
Naivety

Beginning

House 14
FOX

Work
Career
Cunning Nose,
Ears

Delay

House 15
BEAR

Money
Finances
Strength
Power

10 years

House 16
STAR

Wishes
Dreams
Serenity
Happiness

Night

House 17 — STORK

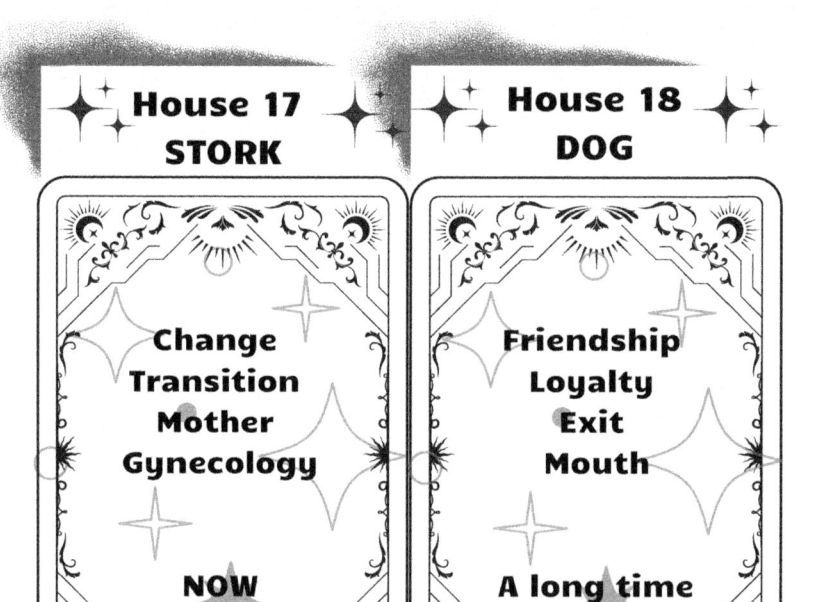

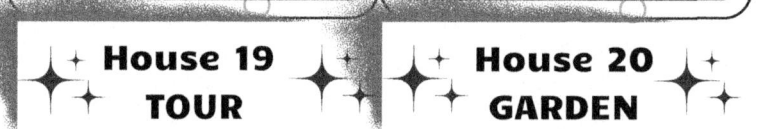

Change
Transition
Mother
Gynecology

NOW

House 18 — DOG

Friendship
Loyalty
Exit
Mouth

A long time

House 19 — TOUR

Isolation
Administration
Institution
Spine

Winter

House 20 — GARDEN

Social Circle
Renown
Nature
Good Health

Long Period

House 21
MONT

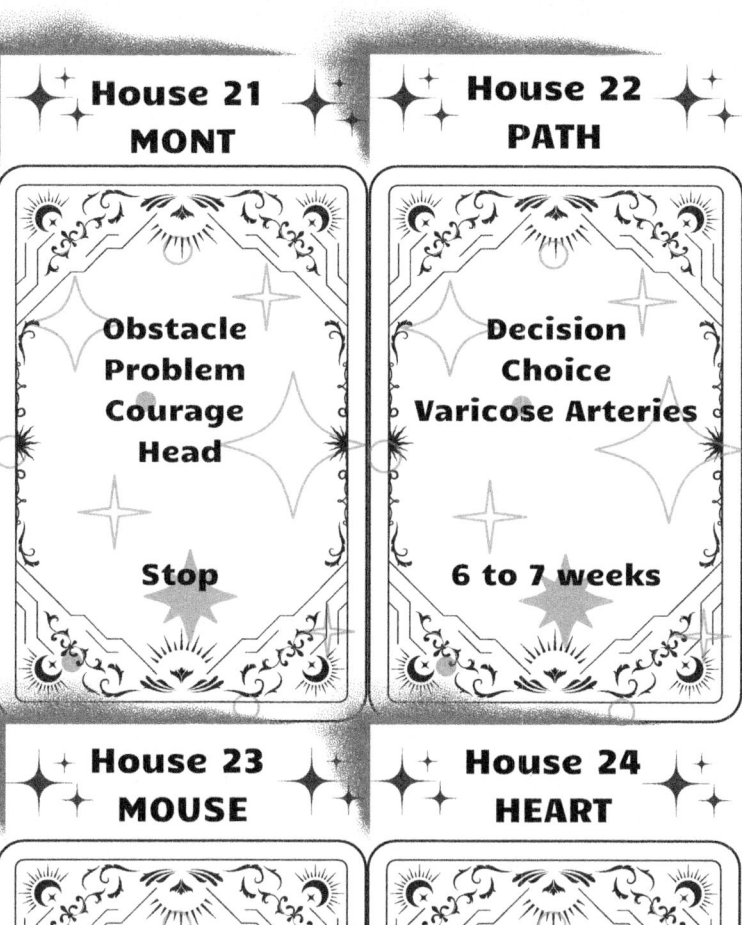

Obstacle
Problem
Courage
Head

Stop

House 22
PATH

Decision
Choice
Varicose Arteries

6 to 7 weeks

House 23
MOUSE

Loss
Flight
Anxiety
Arthritis

Waste of Time

House 24
HEART

Love
Happiness
Sharing
Romance

Spring

House 25 — RING

Contract,
Association
Marriage,
Commitment
Precious object
Chronic illness

7 years old

House 26 — BOOK

Secret
Learnings
Administrative
Paper
Unconscious

Time to Come

House 27 — LETTER

Mail
Writer
Fleeting Sensation

Short Term

House 28 — MISTER

Man
Husband
Consultant

House 29
LADY

Woman
Wife
Consultant

House 30
LIGHT

Joy
Conciliator
Help

Winter

House 31
SUN

Male
Father
Success
Fame

Summer

House 32
MOON

Feminine
Mother
Illusion
Emotions
Introspection

Night

House 33
KEY

Solution
Chance
Essential

House 34
FISH

Abundance
Creativity
Money
Independent profession
Kidneys, bladder

Long term

House 35
ANCHOR

Deep
Attachment
Stability
Hips, Pelvis

A long time

House 36
CROSS

Burden
Trauma
Misfortune
Spirituality
Lower Back

2 weeks

Printed in Great Britain
by Amazon